Everything You Ever Wanted to Know About Minnesota Vikings

© 2017 Ian Carroll

Everything You Ever Wanted to Know About....

Absolutely nothing, because we really don't care...

Everything You Ever Wanted to Know About…

Absolutely nothing, because we really don't care…

Everything You Ever Wanted to Know About...

Absolutely nothing, because we really don't care...

Everything You Ever Wanted to Know About...

Absolutely nothing, because we really don't care...

Everything You Ever Wanted to Know About...

Absolutely nothing, because we really don't care...

Everything You Ever Wanted to Know About...

Absolutely nothing, because we really don't care...

Everything You Ever Wanted to Know About...

Absolutely nothing, because we really don't care...

Everything You Ever Wanted to Know About…

Absolutely nothing, because we really don't care…

Everything You Ever Wanted to Know About...

Absolutely nothing, because we really don't care...

Everything You Ever Wanted to Know About...

Absolutely nothing, because we really don't care...

Everything You Ever Wanted to Know About...

Absolutely nothing, because we really don't care...

Everything You Ever Wanted to Know About…

Absolutely nothing, because we really don't care….

Everything You Ever Wanted to Know About….

Absolutely nothing, because we really don't care…

Everything You Ever Wanted to Know About...

Absolutely nothing, because we really don't care…..

Everything You Ever Wanted to Know About…..

Absolutely nothing, because we really don't care…

Everything You Ever Wanted to Know About...

Absolutely nothing, because we really don't care...

Everything You Ever Wanted to Know About...

Absolutely nothing, because we really don't care...

Everything You Ever Wanted to Know About...

Absolutely nothing, because we really don't care...

Everything You Ever Wanted to Know About…

Absolutely nothing, because we really don't care…

Everything You Ever Wanted to Know About…

Absolutely nothing, because we really don't care…

Everything You Ever Wanted to Know About...

Absolutely nothing, because we really don't care...

Everything You Ever Wanted to Know About...

Absolutely nothing, because we really don't care...

Everything You Ever Wanted to Know About…

Absolutely nothing, because we really don't care…

Everything You Ever Wanted to Know About…

Absolutely nothing, because we really don't care…

Everything You Ever Wanted to Know About...

Absolutely nothing, because we really don't care...

Everything You Ever Wanted to Know About...

Absolutely nothing, because we really don't care...

Everything You Ever Wanted to Know About...

Absolutely nothing, because we really don't care...

Everything You Ever Wanted to Know About...

Absolutely nothing, because we really don't care...

Everything You Ever Wanted to Know About...

Absolutely nothing, because we really don't care...

Everything You Ever Wanted to Know About…

Absolutely nothing, because we really don't care…

Everything You Ever Wanted to Know About...

Absolutely nothing, because we really don't care...

Everything You Ever Wanted to Know About…

Absolutely nothing, because we really don't care…

Everything You Ever Wanted to Know About...

Absolutely nothing, because we really don't care...

Everything You Ever Wanted to Know About…

Absolutely nothing, because we really don't care….

Everything You Ever Wanted to Know About….

Absolutely nothing, because we really don't care…

Everything You Ever Wanted to Know About...

Absolutely nothing, because we really don't care...

Everything You Ever Wanted to Know About...

Absolutely nothing, because we really don't care...

Everything You Ever Wanted to Know About...

Absolutely nothing, because we really don't care...

Everything You Ever Wanted to Know About...

Absolutely nothing, because we really don't care...

Everything You Ever Wanted to Know About....

Absolutely nothing, because we really don't care...

Everything You Ever Wanted to Know About....

Absolutely nothing, because we really don't care...

Everything You Ever Wanted to Know About...

Absolutely nothing, because we really don't care...

Everything You Ever Wanted to Know About...

Absolutely nothing, because we really don't care...

Everything You Ever Wanted to Know About...

Absolutely nothing, because we really don't care...

Everything You Ever Wanted to Know About...

Absolutely nothing, because we really don't care...

Everything You Ever Wanted to Know About…

Absolutely nothing, because we really don't care…..

Everything You Ever Wanted to Know About…..

Absolutely nothing, because we really don't care…

Everything You Ever Wanted to Know About…

Absolutely nothing, because we really don't care…

Everything You Ever Wanted to Know About...

Absolutely nothing, because we really don't care...

Everything You Ever Wanted to Know About...

Absolutely nothing, because we really don't care...

Everything You Ever Wanted to Know About...

Absolutely nothing, because we really don't care...

Everything You Ever Wanted to Know About...

Absolutely nothing, because we really don't care...

Everything You Ever Wanted to Know About...

Absolutely nothing, because we really don't care...

Everything You Ever Wanted to Know About...

Absolutely nothing, because we really don't care...

Everything You Ever Wanted to Know About...

Absolutely nothing, because we really don't care...

Everything You Ever Wanted to Know About...

Absolutely nothing, because we really don't care...

Everything You Ever Wanted to Know About...

Absolutely nothing, because we really don't care...

Everything You Ever Wanted to Know About...

Absolutely nothing, because we really don't care….

Everything You Ever Wanted to Know About…..

Absolutely nothing, because we really don't care…

Everything You Ever Wanted to Know About...

Absolutely nothing, because we really don't care...

Everything You Ever Wanted to Know About...

Absolutely nothing, because we really don't care....

Everything You Ever Wanted to Know About...

Absolutely nothing, because we really don't care...

Everything You Ever Wanted to Know About...

Absolutely nothing, because we really don't care...

Everything You Ever Wanted to Know About...

Absolutely nothing, because we really don't care...

Everything You Ever Wanted to Know About...

Absolutely nothing, because we really don't care...

Everything You Ever Wanted to Know About…

Absolutely nothing, because we really don't care….

Everything You Ever Wanted to Know About....

Absolutely nothing, because we really don't care...

Everything You Ever Wanted to Know About...

Absolutely nothing, because we really don't care...

Everything You Ever Wanted to Know About...

Absolutely nothing, because we really don't care...

Everything You Ever Wanted to Know About...

Absolutely nothing, because we really don't care...

Everything You Ever Wanted to Know About...

Absolutely nothing, because we really don't care...

Everything You Ever Wanted to Know About...

Absolutely nothing, because we really don't care...

Everything You Ever Wanted to Know About…

Absolutely nothing, because we really don't care…

Everything You Ever Wanted to Know About…

Absolutely nothing, because we really don't care…

Everything You Ever Wanted to Know About...

Absolutely nothing, because we really don't care……

Everything You Ever Wanted to Know About…

Absolutely nothing, because we really don't care…

Everything You Ever Wanted to Know About...

Absolutely nothing, because we really don't care...

Everything You Ever Wanted to Know About…

Absolutely nothing, because we really don't care….

Everything You Ever Wanted to Know About...

Absolutely nothing, because we really don't care...

Everything You Ever Wanted to Know About…

Absolutely nothing, because we really don't care…

Everything You Ever Wanted to Know About...

Absolutely nothing, because we really don't care...

Everything You Ever Wanted to Know About...

Absolutely nothing, because we really don't care...

Everything You Ever Wanted to Know About...

Absolutely nothing, because we really don't care...

Everything You Ever Wanted to Know About...

Absolutely nothing, because we really don't care...

Everything You Ever Wanted to Know About...

Absolutely nothing, because we really don't care...

Everything You Ever Wanted to Know About…

Absolutely nothing, because we really don't care…

Everything You Ever Wanted to Know About...

Absolutely nothing, because we really don't care...

Everything You Ever Wanted to Know About...

Absolutely nothing, because we really don't care...

Everything You Ever Wanted to Know About...

Absolutely nothing, because we really don't care...

Everything You Ever Wanted to Know About…

Absolutely nothing, because we really don't care….

Everything You Ever Wanted to Know About….

Absolutely nothing, because we really don't care…

Everything You Ever Wanted to Know About...

Absolutely nothing, because we really don't care...

Everything You Ever Wanted to Know About...

Absolutely nothing, because we really don't care...

Everything You Ever Wanted to Know About…

Absolutely nothing, because we really don't care…

Everything You Ever Wanted to Know About...

Absolutely nothing, because we really don't care...

Everything You Ever Wanted to Know About...

Absolutely nothing, because we really don't care...

Everything You Ever Wanted to Know About…

Absolutely nothing, because we really don't care…

Everything You Ever Wanted to Know About…

Absolutely nothing, because we really don't care…

Everything You Ever Wanted to Know About...

Absolutely nothing, because we really don't care...

Everything You Ever Wanted to Know About…

Absolutely nothing, because we really don't care…

Everything You Ever Wanted to Know About...

Absolutely nothing, because we really don't care...

Everything You Ever Wanted to Know About...

Absolutely nothing, because we really don't care...

Everything You Ever Wanted to Know About...

Absolutely nothing, because we really don't care...

Everything You Ever Wanted to Know About...

Absolutely nothing, because we really don't care...

Everything You Ever Wanted to Know About...

Absolutely nothing, because we really don't care...

Everything You Ever Wanted to Know About...

Absolutely nothing, because we really don't care...

Everything You Ever Wanted to Know About...

Absolutely nothing, because we really don't care...

Everything You Ever Wanted to Know About...

Absolutely nothing, because we really don't care...

Everything You Ever Wanted to Know About...

Absolutely nothing, because we really don't care...

Everything You Ever Wanted to Know About...

Absolutely nothing, because we really don't care...

Everything You Ever Wanted to Know About...

Absolutely nothing, because we really don't care...

Everything You Ever Wanted to Know About…

Absolutely nothing, because we really don't care…

Everything You Ever Wanted to Know About...

Absolutely nothing, because we really don't care...

Everything You Ever Wanted to Know About...

Absolutely nothing, because we really don't care...

Everything You Ever Wanted to Know About...

Absolutely nothing, because we really don't care...

Everything You Ever Wanted to Know About…

Absolutely nothing, because we really don't care…

Everything You Ever Wanted to Know About...

Absolutely nothing, because we really don't care...

Everything You Ever Wanted to Know About...

Absolutely nothing, because we really don't care...

Everything You Ever Wanted to Know About...

Absolutely nothing, because we really don't care...

Everything You Ever Wanted to Know About....

Absolutely nothing, because we really don't care...

Everything You Ever Wanted to Know About…

Absolutely nothing, because we really don't care…..

Everything You Ever Wanted to Know About...

Absolutely nothing, because we really don't care...

Everything You Ever Wanted to Know About...

Absolutely nothing, because we really don't care...

Everything You Ever Wanted to Know About...

Absolutely nothing, because we really don't care...

Everything You Ever Wanted to Know About…

Absolutely nothing, because we really don't care…

Everything You Ever Wanted to Know About...

Absolutely nothing, because we really don't care...

Everything You Ever Wanted to Know About...

Absolutely nothing, because we really don't care...

Everything You Ever Wanted to Know About...

Absolutely nothing, because we really don't care...

Everything You Ever Wanted to Know About...

Absolutely nothing, because we really don't care...

Absolutely nothing at all, because we really don't care...